The
Colonial Cook

Bobbie Kalman & Ellen Brown
Illustrations by Barbara Bedell
 Crabtree Publishing
www.crabtreebooks.com

Created by Bobbie Kalman

Dedicated by Ellen Brown
For my great nephew, Ilan David Dubler-Furman,
who will always be warmed by the hearth of love

Editor-in-Chief
Bobbie Kalman

Writing team
Bobbie Kalman
Ellen Brown

Project editor
Kathryn Smithyman

Editors
Niki Walker
Amanda Bishop
Laurie Thomas

Computer design
Margaret Amy Reiach
Robert MacGregor (cover)

Production coordinator
Heather Fitzpatrick

Photo researchers
Heather Fitzpatrick
Jaimie Nathan

Consultant
Ellen Brown, Founding Food Editor
of *USA Today* and author of several
best-selling cookbooks

Special thanks to
Old Salem, Amanda Vernal and Allison Vernal who
appear on pages 24-27, Margaret Nacsa, Fort George,
Peter Crabtree, Marc Crabtree

Photographs
Colonial Williamsburg Foundation: pages 11, 14 (top),
15, 20, 21, 30
Photos courtesy of Old Salem, Winston-Salem, N.C.:
title page
Claude Moore Colonial Farm: pages 18, 19
Marc Crabtree at Fort George: page 14 (bottom)
Bobbie Kalman: pages 24, 26, 27

Illustrations
All illustrations by Barbara Bedell except
the following:
Margaret Amy Reiach: page 15, 23 (peel and whisk),
28 (top left)
Tiffany Wybouw: page 16 (middle right), 17 (top left),
19 (bottom right), 24, 25, 26 (bottom left), 31 (top)
Bonna Rouse: page 26 (top)
Halina Below-Spada: page 18
Antoinette "Cookie" Bortolon: page 9 (top right),
16 (bottom left)
Trevor Morgan: page 9 (top left)

Crabtree Publishing Company

www.crabtreebooks.com   1-800-387-7650

PMB 16A	612 Welland Ave.	73 Lime Walk
350 Fifth Ave.	St. Catharines	Headington
Suite 3308	Ontario	Oxford
New York, NY	Canada	OX3 7AD
10118	L2M 5V6	United Kingdom

Cataloging in Publication Data
Kalman, Bobbie
      The colonial cook / Bobbie Kalman and Ellen Brown;
illustrated by Barbara Bedell.
            p. cm. -- (Colonial people)
      Includes index.
      Discusses the foods, methods, equipment, and places used by
cooks in colonial America.
      ISBN 0-7787-0748-2 (RLB) -- ISBN 0-7787-0794-6 (pbk.)
      1. Cookery, American--History--Juvenile literature. 2. United
States--History--Colonial period, ca. 1600-1775--Juvenile literature.
[1. Cookery, American. 2. United States--History--Colonial period,
ca. 1600-1775.]   I. Bedell, Barbara, ill. II. Title.
   TX715 .K127496 2002
   641.5973'09'032--dc21
                                                                    2001037215

Contents

Who was the colonial cook?

In many **colonial** homes, the woman of the family ran the household. She was responsible for preparing, preserving, and cooking foods. If she had daughters, they helped her with these chores. The daughters peeled potatoes, gathered eggs, **churned** butter, helped bake bread, and brought in water from the well. In wealthier households, the woman of the house did not do the cooking herself. She planned meals and supervised the servants who prepared and cooked the food. Most colonial cooks were women, but some were men. Both men and women worked as cooks and bakers in **taverns** and on **plantations**. Unmarried men or men whose wives had died also cooked meals.

Indentured servants

In the 1600s, people called **indentured servants** worked as cooks in many colonial homes. Most of these servants were people who wanted to move from Europe to the **colonies** but could not afford the costly sea voyage. They made **indentures**, or contracts, with employers who paid for their trip. In exchange, indentured servants agreed to work without pay until their debt was repaid. Most indentures lasted five to seven years.

Slaves in the kitchen

In later colonial times, many wealthy families purchased **slaves** to work in their homes, fields, and shops. Slaves were people who were brought from Africa against their will and sold as property. They were forced to work without pay. Slave women often worked as cooks in large family homes and on plantations. A slave cook not only prepared meals for her master's family and guests, but she also had to cook meals for her own family.

Slave children helped prepare meals. They shucked corn, swept floors, washed dishes, and brought in firewood from the woodpile. They also fetched water from an outdoor well.

The cooking fire

In early colonial times, homes were fairly small. Most houses had only one room in which an entire family lived, ate, and slept. A fireplace in the center of the room provided heat, light, and a place to cook. Even in homes with more than one room, family members often gathered around the kitchen fireplace.

A big fireplace

A colonial fireplace was large and open. A cook could hang two or three big iron **kettles**, or pots, over the fire at the same time. She cooked most foods in these kettles. Sometimes she burned her fingers as she added logs to the fire or stirred the contents of a kettle.

Using a lugpole

The early colonial cook had an especially dangerous job! She hung her cooking kettle from a **lugpole**, which was a branch cut from a young, green tree. For outdoor cooking, as shown on the right, the lugpole rested on two young tree trunks. Indoors, its ends fitted into small holes in the sides of the fireplace so that the pole stretched over the fire.

Dangerous spills

Both indoors and out, the lugpole could catch fire or snap when it became dry. If a pole snapped while a kettle was hanging on it, the heavy pot crashed down and spilled its steaming contents—sometimes on the cook.

Safer kitchens

Cooking was safer in later colonial kitchens. The lugpole was replaced by an iron bar called a **crane**. The crane swung out of the fireplace and away from the flames so that cooks did not have to reach over the fire to stir food. A cook used metal hooks called **trammels** to hang pots from the crane. By using trammels of different lengths, she moved a pot closer to or farther from the fire. Even with a crane, the cook had to be careful around a fire, especially in a long dress!

Pots, pans, and gadgets

Pots and pans were expensive. Some cooks owned several, but many did all their cooking in one or two pots. Cookware was designed to cook a variety of foods in different ways. Many pots and pans were made of iron, so they were sturdy enough to hang over the fire or sit among the burning coals without cracking or melting. The pictures on this page show a few of the basic kettles and pans that cooks used every day.

Soups and stews were cooked in a large iron kettle.

*This **spider** had three legs—not eight! A spider was a frying pan with legs that raised its cooking surface above the coals. The long handle allowed the cook to move the pan without putting her hands near the fire.*

A kettle with a spout was used to boil water for tea and other hot drinks.

The cook filled this iron basket with potatoes and placed it inside a large kettle of water to boil. To make roasted potatoes, the cook hung the basket above the fire.

*The colonial cook placed the **Dutch oven**, or bake kettle, into the fireplace coals. She then scooped hot coals on top of the lid as well so the food would cook evenly on all sides. The cook baked hams, casseroles, and cakes in the Dutch oven.*

Kitchen gadgets

A **gadget** is a useful tool, utensil, or machine that performs a simple job such as cutting. A **coffee mill**, for example, is a gadget that grinds coffee beans. Colonial gadgets were not powered by electricity.

*In colonial times, white sugar was sold as a solid cone wrapped in paper. A metal sugar **nipper**, or cutter, was used to snip off pieces of sugar as they were needed.*

*This handy **waffle iron** made delicious waffles!*

*When colonial cooks needed to make a fire hotter, they blew air onto it using a **bellows**. A bellows was a leather bag attached to two wooden paddles. Squeezing the paddles forced air out of the bag and onto the coals of the fire.*

To make toast, the cook placed slices of bread between the metal bars of this toaster and then put the toaster in front of the fire. When one side of the toast was done, she turned the bread to toast the other side.

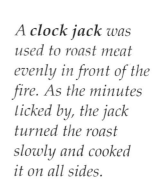

*A **clock jack** was used to roast meat evenly in front of the fire. As the minutes licked by, the jack turned the roast slowly and cooked it on all sides.*

spit

*Another way to roast meat was to put it on a **spit** and slowly turn it over the fire. Some cooks used dog power to turn the roast. A **dog wheel** was attached to the spit, and as the dog ran, it turned the meat over and over. As a result, the roast cooked thoroughly.*

Big
House

kitchen house

The kitchen house

In large homes and on plantations, the kitchen was a separate building. It was often connected to the **Big House**, or main house, by a **breezeway**, or covered walkway. Having a separate kitchen kept heat and cooking smells away from the living areas. It was also safer. If the kitchen caught fire, the flames could be put out before they spread to the main house.

Families who lived in places with cold winters often had two kitchens. In summer, they cooked in a separate building called a **summer kitchen** or at an outdoor fireplace or oven. During winter, they used the fireplace inside the main house, since doing so helped keep the entire house warm.

The dining room

Families with kitchen houses ate their meals in dining rooms. From the dining room, people did not have to see or hear the cook preparing meals. They simply waited for servants or slaves to bring their food from the kitchen.

A warm place to sleep

If the cook was a servant or slave, she and her family often lived in the kitchen house, in a room above or next to the kitchen. The cook was the first to rise in the morning. She started the fire.

The pantry

The kitchen house had another room called a **pantry**, which was used to store pots, pans, serving dishes, and food. The hot kitchen was not a good place to store foods that spoiled easily. Such foods, along with **flour**, herbs, and spices, were stored in the pantry, where they were out of the cook's way until she needed them. Bundles of corn and herbs hung in the pantry to dry. Some cooks also hung fish and game birds from the ceiling until it was time to cook them.

Work in the dependencies

Some colonists built small buildings, called **dependencies**, in which they prepared or stored different kinds of foods. Dependencies were named for the purposes they served. Most were built to keep foods fresh, dry, and away from animals. When cooks were not busy preparing meals, they had plenty of work to do in the dependencies.

The smoke house

The cook used the **smoke house** to **cure**, or preserve, meats and fish over a smoky fire. Smoke from different types of wood flavored the meat as well as curing it. The cook hung pieces of meat and fish from the rafters and then built a fire in a pit below the smoke house. The smoke rose and filled the small building, since there was no chimney through which it could escape.

The chicken coop

Many families raised chickens. They kept the chickens in a **coop**, where the birds laid eggs in wooden boxes filled with straw. Colonial cooks used eggs in many of their **dishes**.

The root cellar

The **root cellar** was not a separate building. It was dug into the earth beneath the house. Cooks stored root vegetables such as beets, carrots, and potatoes in the cool cellar. They covered them with straw or sand to keep them from spoiling.

The spring house

Colonial homes did not have indoor plumbing. People gathered water from streams, lakes, and springs. Those who lived near mountain springs also used the cold water to keep foods such as butter and cheese from spoiling. They placed covered **crocks**, or clay pots, of food right into the water. Many built **spring houses** over the springs to keep animals away from the food.

The well house

If there was no water source nearby, a family dug a deep well to find water in the ground. Many wells had roofs above them to keep leaves from falling into the water. Some families built **well houses** around their wells. The cold water kept the whole building cool, so milk and butter were often stored there if the family had no dairy.

Making butter and cheese

Butter and cheese were eaten almost every day, so colonial cooks made them frequently. Both foods started as milk. To make butter, the cook left a crock of milk in a cool place overnight to allow the cream to rise to the top. In the morning, she skimmed off the cream, put it in a churn, and pumped the churn's **dasher**, or paddle, up and down. When small clumps of butter formed, the cook removed the butter and rinsed and salted it. She then put the butter into a mold to shape it. The liquid left in the churn was **buttermilk**. Cheese was made by **curdling** milk, or separating it into solid lumps called **curds**, and liquid called **whey**. The curds could be eaten soft like cottage cheese, or the cook could press them together to form a harder cheese.

The dairy

The **dairy** was built in a cool, shady area and had a stone floor that helped keep the building cool. This dependency often had two rooms—one for making butter and cheese and one for storing them.

Foods grown and raised

Most colonial families grew grains, fruits, and vegetables and raised animals for meat, milk, and eggs. Colonial cooks made all their meals from scratch, using ingredients they grew and prepared themselves.

grew many of their own vegetables in a garden behind their home. Common garden crops included beets, cabbages, beans, carrots, and potatoes.

Grown from seeds

Many **colonists** brought seeds with them from Europe. From the seeds, they grew apple, pear, cherry, and plum trees. Cooks also saved the seeds from vegetables and fruits and planted them the following spring. Even people who lived in towns and cities

Preserving foods

Cooks preserved many fresh fruits and vegetables so they could eat them year-round. They cooked some fruits with sugar to make **preserves** such as jams, jellies, and marmalades. They dried or **pickled** other fruits and vegetables. Cooks could also buy jars of marmalade, jam, and pickles in town shops.

Meat, milk, and eggs

Many colonists raised chickens, which provided eggs. Families also had at least one cow. Cows produced milk and cream, which cooks made into butter, cheese, and buttermilk.

Sheep and pigs

Much of the meat eaten by the colonists came from pigs and sheep. When colonists butchered pigs, they made hams, bacon, and sausages from the meat. They also boiled down pig fat to make **tallow**, which they used to make soap and candles. Sheep provided milk, meat, and wool, which was spun into yarn and woven into cloth or knit into sweaters.

Hunting and fishing

Colonists could not butcher all their animals for meat. They needed live animals for eggs, milk, and wool. For extra meat, men and boys often hunted deer, squirrels, and rabbits and trapped turkeys and pheasants. They also caught fish in rivers, lakes, and in the ocean.

Preserving meat

On farms, cooks had several ways of preserving meat to make it last for months. Large hunks of meat were often smoked or stored in barrels of **brine**, or salty water. Cooks also sliced meat into thin strips and dried it to make **jerky**. In larger towns, colonists could buy fresh meat and fish at butcher shops and markets.

Colonists raised sheep and other animals for food. Sheep also provided the colonists with wool.

From grains to bread

The granary was a small storage building. It was built on posts that raised it off the ground to keep the corn dry and prevent animals from getting in.

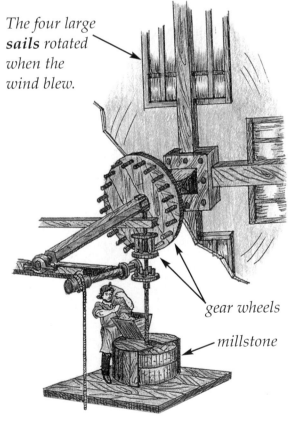

The four large **sails** rotated when the wind blew.

gear wheels

millstone

The sails of the windmill were attached to **gear wheels**, which turned the top millstone inside the mill. The grain was ground between it and the bottom millstone, which did not move.

Grains such as oats, barley, corn, and wheat were an important part of the colonial diet. Most families grew these crops. After they **harvested**, or cut down the grains, they stored them in a **granary**.

Flour from grains

Colonial cooks used flour to make baked goods such as bread, cakes, pies, and biscuits. Flour is made by grinding grains into a fine powder. In early colonial homes, mothers and daughters pounded grain into flour using a **mortar** and **pestle**. In large households, servants or slaves did the grinding because it was such hard work. It took a long time to pound enough grain for a single loaf of bread!

Gristmills

As towns grew, **gristmills** were often built to grind grain into flour. Some gristmills used the power of moving water to grind grain. **Windmills** used the power of the wind. The wind or water turned the sails, which then turned a large, heavy millstone. The turning stone ground grains into flour.

Bread ingredients

The main ingredient in bread is flour.

Flour is combined with **yeast** to make the bread dough rise. Yeast is a tiny living thing that feeds on the flour in bread dough and then gives off a gas called **carbon dioxide.** The carbon dioxide expands inside the dough and makes it **rise**, or expand. Colonial cooks skimmed yeast from the top of beer or ale, mixed it with flour, and then added water and salt to make bread dough.

Baking bread

Baking bread involved many steps. After the cook made the dough, she **kneaded**, or worked, it by hand. She then covered the dough and set it aside to let it rise. When it doubled in size, she punched the dough to get the air out, shaped it into loaves, and placed it in a **bread oven**. The bread oven was built into the side of the fireplace. Before putting in the loaves, the cook placed hot coals inside the oven to heat it. The oven held the heat of the coals and baked the bread.

*The cook used a paddle called a **baking peel** to slide bread in and out of the oven. Many colonial cooks spent one day each week baking breads, pies, and pastries. Baked goods were eaten at every meal.*

17

Preparing for the day

In order to have the morning meal ready on time, the cook began preparing it before dawn. She first had to start the fire by stirring up the previous day's coals and laying wood over them. She kept the coals hot overnight by burying them in ash. Milk and eggs were both eaten at breakfast, so the cook also had to milk the cow and gather the eggs early in the morning.

If the cook did not have children or servants to help her, she fetched water from a well, gathered eggs, and milked the cow herself. The cook brought in some milk for breakfast and left the rest in the dairy. She also picked some fresh herbs from the garden. If there was any meat left over from the previous evening, the cook served it for breakfast with bread or eggs.

Morning work

While the cook was busy preparing breakfast, other family members were doing morning chores such as chopping wood, feeding the animals, and cleaning the barns. People took advantage of the cooler mornings to get work done. By the time breakfast was ready, everyone was hungry!

Pies and puddings

Pies and puddings were served at almost every meal, but they were breakfast favorites. Breakfast pies had fruit fillings. Puddings were made by boiling roughly ground grain with milk and butter. The cook added cream, maple syrup, and extra butter to a breakfast pudding. The recipe on the right is for Hasty Pudding. Before you start making it, read pages 22 and 23!

Busy all day

The cook did not rest after breakfast. Meals could take several hours to make, so the cook immediately started preparing the food she would serve at the other meals that day. While the food cooked, she washed the pots and dishes and cleaned the kitchen. During the afternoon, she did various chores such as gathering vegetables and fruits from the garden, preserving various foods, and making butter.

Hasty Pudding

Preparation time: 15 minutes
Cooking time: 25 minutes
Servings: 4
Tools: **saucepan**, measuring cups, measuring spoons, wire **whisk**

Ingredients

- 2 cups (500 ml) milk
- ½ cup (125 ml) cornmeal
- ¼ cup (62 ml) maple syrup
- 2 tablespoons (30 ml) butter
- ½ teaspoon (2.5 ml) salt

Method

1. Pour the milk into a saucepan and bring it to a boil over medium heat.
2. Using a wire whisk, slowly stir in the cornmeal and blend until the mixture is smooth.
3. Cook the mixture over low heat, stirring constantly until it is thick.
4. Stir in the maple syrup, butter, and salt. Cook the mixture over low heat until the butter has melted.
5. Cover the pot, turn off the stove, and allow the pudding to sit for 5 minutes.
6. Serve the pudding hot with a little butter, milk, and maple syrup on top.

Dinnertime!

After breakfast, everyone worked until early afternoon, when it was time to eat again. Today we call our midday meal "lunch," but the colonists called it "dinner." Dinner was the biggest meal of the day. In most homes, the cook prepared one or two main dishes for this meal. In wealthier homes, dinner could include eight or nine dishes.

A cook often served stew for dinner. She could leave it to cook unattended while she did other chores. To make a stew, the cook boiled meat in a kettle. Later in the morning, she added whatever vegetables were available.

Delicious desserts

Everyone loved the sweet dessert served at the end of the meal. Desserts such as fruit pies and **crisps** were made with fresh or dried fruits. Fruits were also used to make ciders, juices, and a refreshing drink called **shrub**. (See page 27 for the recipe.)

Dinner is served!

Wealthy families gathered for dinner in the dining room, where servants or slaves served them several platters of food. Their dinners included many of the same dishes that other families ate at midday.

Formal dining

On special occasions, or when guests were present, the cook prepared foods that took extra time and effort. She trimmed pies with braided dough and sprinkled cakes with sugar. She served these special meals on the family's best dishes. Some wealthy families owned fine dinnerware brought from Europe.

The cook made sure that the food looked beautiful and tasted delicious when it was served to guests.

Not as fancy

Early colonial families and less wealthy families ate meals at rough wooden tables. They ate from **trenchers** using wooden spoons. Trenchers were bowls carved from blocks of wood. Sometimes the trenchers were carved right into the tabletops, as shown in the picture on the right. If there were not enough trenchers for everyone, mothers and daughters ate after the fathers and sons had finished.

Safety tips and cooking terms

The recipes in this book are for dishes similar to those made by colonial cooks. Colonial cooks made everything from scratch, but you do not have to. The recipes we have included use some frozen or canned foods. Colonial cooks used the kitchen tools found on pages 8-9, but with the help of an adult, you can use a blender, mixer, and food processor to prepare the recipes on the following pages.

Receipts, or recipes, were used by some colonial women, but many women could not read or write. They learned how to cook when they were girls by watching and helping their mothers.

Safety tips

- Make sure you have an adult with you while you are working in the kitchen.

- Before handling food, wash and dry your hands. Always wash your hands after handling eggs or raw meat.

- Be sure to wash all vegetables and fruits before you cook or eat them.

- Turn the handles of pots and pans away from the edge of the stove so you do not accidentally knock them and spill hot liquid on yourself or others.

- Always wear oven mitts when you handle anything in the oven.

- If your hair is long, tie it back so that it does not touch the food or get caught while you work.

Cautions

When you see the following symbols beside a recipe, ask an adult to help you:

This recipe has ingredients that need to be chopped or sliced with a sharp knife.

This recipe has ingredients that need to be fried in hot oil or butter on top of a stove.

Cooking terms

The pictures below illustrate the terms used in the recipes. The glossary on page 32 defines other terms that you might need to know.

The recipes also use some short forms for measurements. For example, the letter "l" stands for liter and "ml" stands for milliliter.

dice: *cut food into small cubes*

slice: *cut food into small, even pieces*

core: *remove seeds and stem from fruit*

grate: *rub ingredient against grater*

peel: *slide peeler over fruit to remove peel*

shred: *cut into long, narrow strips*

whisk: *beat with whisk to make mixture fluffy*

rub in: *add ingredient by rubbing between fingers*

blend: *add ingredient while stirring*

beat: *use mixer to stir quickly*

simmer: *allow liquid to bubble slightly*

toothpick test: *check to see if food is baked*

Try these dinner dishes

A colonial cook often served a meat dish such as stew, roasted chicken, or baked ham for dinner, but she also prepared side dishes as part of the meal. She served bread, biscuits, or muffins such as the Apple Cheddar Muffins shown left. After the meal, she dished out a delicious dessert such as Cranberry Apple Crisp. She also served fresh fruit or a fruit preserve such as Spiced Pears, shown below. You can try some colonial recipes in your own kitchen. Before you start, review the safety and cooking tips on pages 22 and 23!

Spiced Pears
Preparation time: 15 minutes
Cool for 8 hours or overnight.
Servings: 6-8
Tools: saucepan, 1-quart (1-liter) jar with a lid

Ingredients
- one 28-ounce (796 ml) can pear halves, drained, or 6 fresh pears, peeled, cored, and cut into halves
- 1½ cups (375 ml) honey
- ½ cup (125 ml) vinegar
- 2 cinnamon sticks
- 3 whole cloves

Method
1. Place the pear halves in a clean jar.
2. In a saucepan, blend the honey and vinegar and add spices. Heat to boiling.
3. Pour the liquid over the pears and let it cool. Cover. Refrigerate at least 8 hours.

Cranberry Apple Crisp

Preparation time: 15 minutes
Cooking time: 1 hour
Servings: 8
Tools: 2 mixing bowls, 8-inch (20 cm) square baking dish, measuring cups and spoons

Topping ingredients
- 1 cup (250 ml) all-purpose flour
- ²/₃ cup (165 ml) firmly packed brown sugar
- ¹/₂ cup (125 ml) old-fashioned oats
- ¹/₂ teaspoon (2.5 ml) salt
- ¹/₂ cup (125 ml) unsalted butter

Filling ingredients
- 7 large firm apples (peeled, cored, and diced)
- 1 cup (250 ml) fresh or frozen cranberries
- ¹/₂ cup (125 ml) white sugar
- ¹/₂ teaspoon (2.5 ml) all-purpose flour
- ¹/₂ teaspoon (2.5 ml) ground cinnamon
- ¹/₂ teaspoon (2.5 ml) ground ginger

Method
1. **Preheat** oven to 350°F (180°C). **Grease** baking dish.
2. For the topping, blend the cup of flour, brown sugar, oats, and salt in a mixing bowl.
3. Cut the butter into small pieces. Using your fingertips, rub it into the topping mixture until the mixture looks crumbly.
4. To make the filling, place the diced apple, cranberries, white sugar, ¹/₂ teaspoon flour, and spices into another mixing bowl. Stir until the fruit is coated.
5. Pour the filling into the baking dish.
6. Sprinkle the topping mixture evenly over the filling.
7. Place the baking dish on a baking sheet and bake one hour or until the topping is golden and the juices bubble.
8. Cool at least 20 minutes before serving. Serve with whipped cream or ice cream.

Apple Cheddar Muffins

Preparation time: 15 minutes
Cooking time: 20-25 minutes
Servings: 12 muffins
Tools: muffin tin, cheese grater, electric mixer, 2 mixing bowls, measuring cups and spoons

Ingredients
- 1¹/₂ cups (375 ml) all-purpose flour
- ¹/₂ cup (125 ml) cornmeal
- 1¹/₂ teaspoons (7.5 ml) baking powder
- ¹/₂ teaspoon (2.5 ml) baking soda
- 1 teaspoon (5 ml) salt
- 1 cup (250 ml) coarsely grated cheddar
- ¹/₂ cup (125 ml) butter
- ²/₃ cup (165 ml) granulated sugar
- 2 large eggs
- 2-3 apples (peeled, cored, and diced or grated)

Method
1. Preheat oven to 350°F (180°C). Grease muffin tin or line it with 12 cupcake papers.
2. In a large mixing bowl, combine flour, cornmeal, baking powder, baking soda, and salt. Add the grated cheddar to the **dry mixture** and stir.
3. In a separate bowl, beat the butter and sugar with an electric mixer. Continue beating as you add the eggs, one at a time.
4. Stir the diced or grated apples into the **wet mixture**.
5. Add the wet mixture to the dry mixture all at once and stir until the dry ingredients are moistened.
6. Fill the muffin cups about ²/₃ full and bake 20 minutes. Do a **toothpick test** to be sure the muffins are done.

Leftovers for supper

The evening meal, called **supper**, was a simple meal. The cook usually prepared it using the leftovers from dinner. Using leftovers saved time, since the cook did not have to prepare a totally new meal. It also ensured that no food was wasted. Some cooks served Hasty Pudding with gravy as a supper dish or used leftover vegetables and meat to make Creamy Chicken on Biscuits, shown below. Try these recipes after you have read pages 22-23.

Creamy Chicken on Biscuits

Preparation time: 15 minutes
Cooking time: 10 minutes
Servings: 6
Tools: sharp knife, measuring cup and spoons, saucepan, long-handled spoon, cutting board dusted with flour, rolling pin, ungreased cookie sheet, a food processor

Ingredients

- 1 small onion, diced
- 2 cups (500 ml) cooked chicken meat sliced into small pieces
- 1 cup (250 ml) sliced mushrooms
- one 10-ounce (284 ml) can chicken gravy
- $\frac{1}{4}$ cup (63 ml) chopped parsley
- $\frac{1}{2}$ cup (125 ml) milk
- 1 tablespoon (15 ml) vegetable oil

Method

1. In a saucepan over medium heat, fry the onion in oil until it looks clear.
2. Add parsley, mushrooms, and chicken and mix together with a long-handled spoon.
3. Pour in the chicken gravy and milk and blend the ingredients.
4. Turn down the heat and simmer the mixture until it is bubbling hot.
5. Split a biscuit open on your plate and spoon the creamy mixture over it. Yum!

Making the biscuits

1. Mix $2\frac{1}{2}$ cups (550 ml) biscuit mix with a $\frac{1}{2}$ cup (125 ml) of milk in a food processor until the ingredients form a dough.
2. Roll out the dough to a $\frac{1}{2}$ inch (1 cm) thickness and cut out biscuits with a glass.
3. Bake the biscuits on an ungreased cookie sheet in a preheated oven at 450°F (230°C) for 8 to 10 minutes or until they are golden.

Hearty Soup

Preparation time: 30 minutes
Cooking time: 60 minutes
Servings: 10-12
Tools: sharp knife, large saucepan with
    lid, long-handled spoon, measuring
    cups and measuring spoons

Ingredients:

- 2 leeks or 1 onion
- 2 celery stalks or 1 green pepper
- 6 carrots or 4 parsnips
- 2 cups (500 ml) fresh spinach
- 2 tablespoons (30 ml) butter
- 4 cups (1 liter) water
- one 28-ounce can (796 ml)
  stewed tomatoes
- 2 cups (500 ml) vegetable or
  chicken broth
- 1 cup (250 ml) green peas
- ½ teaspoon (2.5 ml) thyme
- salt and pepper

*Any vegetable can be added to this soup.
Root vegetables should be added with the
carrots. Dried beans, peas, and lentils
should be cooked before they are added.
Canned or frozen vegetables should be
added in the last ten minutes of cooking.
This soup tastes great served with the
biscuits shown on page 26.*

Method:

1. Wash the vegetables. (Leeks are very
   sandy and should be washed well.)
2. Cut the leeks or onion into small pieces.
   Chop the celery and carrots and other
   vegetables. Tear the spinach using your
   hands. Set these vegetables aside.
3. Melt the butter in a large saucepan.
   Add the carrots, leeks, and celery.
   Cover the pan with a lid and cook
   the vegetables over low heat for 10
   minutes, stirring occasionally with
   a long-handled spoon.
4. Add the water, tomatoes, broth, and
   thyme. Bring the soup to a boil. Reduce
   the heat and simmer for about 20 to 30
   minutes, until the vegetables are tender.
5. Add the peas and spinach to the soup.
   Season the soup with salt and pepper.
   Simmer for another 10 minutes.

Shrub

Shrub is a quick and refreshing dessert
drink. Colonists made shrub with the
juice of various fruits, such as cranberries
and peaches. Use your favorite juice and
sherbet flavors to make your shrub.

Ingredients:

- cranberry juice or a tropical juice blend
- raspberry or lemon sherbet
- sprig of mint, slice of lime (if desired)

Method:

1. Pour juice in a glass until it is ⅔ full.
2. Scoop out some sherbet and drop it
   into the juice.
3. Place a slice of lime on the side of the
   glass and serve the shrub topped with
   a sprig of mint.

Native American gifts of food

The first colonists could not have survived without the help of Native Americans. Native Americans knew about the land and everything that lived and grew on it. They taught the colonists how to fish in streams, hunt and trap animals, and grow crops such as pumpkins and sunflowers. Native Americans showed colonists which fruits, seeds, nuts, and mushrooms were safe to eat, and which plants could be boiled to make beverages or medicines. They also taught colonists how to make jerky by drying strips of meat in the sun. Jerky was especially useful for travelers, since it took up little room and lasted a long time.

An important grain

The most important food Native Americans introduced to colonists was corn. Colonists used this grain in many ways. They ate corn on the cob, heated the kernels to make popcorn, and ground dried corn into cornmeal, which they used to make breads and puddings.

Corn, beans, and squash

Native Americans taught colonists to plant beans and squash between rows of cornstalks. The stalks acted as posts for the bean vines to climb. The squash plants kept the ground shaded and moist so the corn and beans could grow.

Maple Pumpkin Pie
Preparation time: 10 minutes
Cooking time: 1 hour, 15 minutes
Servings: 8
Tools: fork, mixing bowl, electric mixer

Ingredients
- 1 frozen deep-dish pie crust, thawed
- 2 large eggs
- ½ cup (125 ml) whipping cream
- ½ cup (125 ml) maple syrup
- 2 tablespoons (30 ml) flour
- 1½ teaspoons (7.5 ml) pumpkin-pie spice
- ½ (2.5 ml) teaspoon salt
- one 28 fluid ounce can (796 ml) pure pumpkin
- ¼ cup (60 ml) dark brown sugar

Method
1. Preheat oven to 350°F (180°C). Poke the thawed crust all over with a fork. Put the crust into the oven and bake for 10 minutes. Remove it from the oven and let it cool in the pan.
2. In a large bowl, blend the eggs, cream, maple syrup, flour, pumpkin-pie spice, and salt using an electric mixer.
3. Add the pumpkin and brown sugar to the mixture and blend.
4. Pour the filling into the cooled crust.
5. Put the pie into the oven and bake it for 1 hour and 15 minutes or until the filling is puffed up.
6. Remove the pie from the oven and let it cool 10 minutes. Serve the pie warm, topped with whipped cream or vanilla ice cream.

Sweet treats

Native Americans taught the northern colonists how to tap maple trees and boil down the **sap**. The boiled sap thickened into maple syrup and maple sugar, which the colonists used to sweeten foods and drinks. Maple syrup and maple sugar often replaced white sugar in colonial kitchens, since white sugar was very expensive.

Colonial families used maple syrup to sweeten all kinds of foods. Sugar was expensive and not always available. It was used mostly by wealthy families.

African American cooking

African American slaves had a different diet than that of their masters. Most slaves relied on weekly rations of food given to them by their masters. The rations usually included the parts of vegetables that the master's family would not eat, such as turnip greens, and animal parts such as ears, feet, snouts, tails, and small intestines. Slaves also received some corn, cornmeal, salt, and rice.

In their spare time, slaves caught raccoons and opossums and grew small gardens with vegetable seeds that some had brought from Africa. The vegetables included black-eyed peas, eggplant, okra, and peanuts. Slave women who worked as cooks slowly introduced foods and flavors from Africa to their masters. They also changed their own recipes from home to include local foods.

Simple, hearty meals

Since slaves spent their days working in the fields or at the master's house, they did not have time to prepare fancy meals. Mothers made soup or stew in the morning or the night before and left it to simmer in the fireplace during the day. Many slaves cooked **hoecakes** or **ashcakes** to go with their meals. These small cakes were made by mixing cornmeal with salt, water, and fat and shaping the mixture into small patties. Hoecakes were cooked on the blade of a hoe, over an open fire. Ashcakes were cooked right in the coals and were washed before they were eaten.

Good for the soul

Unlike their masters, who ate their main meal at midday, most slaves ate their biggest meal at suppertime. Slaves looked forward to supper, since they finally had time to spend with their family and friends after a hard day's work. Away from the master, the slaves were free to talk, laugh, sing, and tell stories. They felt their evening meal was as good for their bodies as it was for their souls. For this reason, African American dishes came to be known as "soul food."

To make Peanut Soup, right, colonial cooks roasted peanuts in a skillet and then ground them into pieces. You can use peanut butter.

Slave mothers and daughters ground corn into cornmeal using a mortar and pestle. They also ground peanuts for Peanut Soup in the same way.

Peanut Soup

Preparation time: 10 minutes
Cooking time: 15 minutes
Servings: 6
Tools: medium saucepan, long-handled spoon, wire whisk, measuring cups and spoons

Ingredients

- 2 tablespoons (30 ml) butter
- 3 tablespoons (45 ml) flour
- 3 cups (750 ml) chicken broth
- 1 cup (250 ml) peanut butter
- 1 cup (250 ml) whole milk
- ½ teaspoon (2.5 ml) salt
- ½ teaspoon (2.5 ml) black pepper

Method

1. Melt butter in the saucepan over low heat. Blend in the flour and stir for a minute. Raise heat to medium-high.
2. Add ½ cup of broth to the pan. Keep stirring as it boils, slowly adding the rest of the broth. Reduce heat to low and simmer the mixture for 3 minutes.
3. Whisk in the peanut butter and milk. Beat until the mixture is smooth. Add salt and pepper. Simmer for 2 more minutes.
4. Serve the soup hot.

Glossary

churn (n) A wooden container with a paddle used to make butter; (v) The act of stirring cream to make butter

colonial Relating to living in a colony or to a period when European countries ruled North America

colonist A person who lives in a colony

colony An area ruled by a faraway country, such as England or France

crisp A fruit dessert with a crunchy topping

cure To preserve food by smoking, salting, or hanging it to dry in a warm place

dish A recipe or serving of food

dry mixture The combined dry ingredients in a recipe, such as flour or sugar

grease To coat the surface of a pan with oil or melted butter

jerky Thin strips of meat dried in the sun

mortar A container in which substances such as grains are pounded into a powder

pestle A tool used for pounding

pickle To preserve food in vinegar or salty water

plantation A large farm with one main crop

preheat To turn on an oven and allow it to reach a certain temperature

preserve To treat or store food in a way that stops it from spoiling

preserves Fruit cooked with sugar and sealed in a jar to prevent it from spoiling

sap Liquid inside a tree that carries food to its parts

saucepan A small, deep pan with a handle

simmer To heat liquid until it bubbles slowly and lightly

slave A person treated as property and forced to work for no pay

tavern A public place where meals and drinks are sold and rooms are rented

toothpick test A method of testing whether baked goods are done by poking a toothpick into the center and pulling it out; food is baked if the toothpick is clean

wet mixture The combined moist ingredients in a recipe, such as milk, butter, and eggs,

whisk (n) A utensil used to whip food; (v) The act of whipping food

Index

1 2 3 4 5 6 7 8 9 0 Printed in the U.S.A. 1 0 9 8 7 6 5 4 3 2